A look at Morgan's Raiders and their dash through Meigs County, Ohio and culminating in

The Battle of Buffington Island

Accounts, Notes, Telegrams, Diary Entries, Facts and Pictures

Created by C. Stephen Badgley
Badgley Publishing Company

and

Dedicated to all the fine people of Meigs County, Ohio

Copyright © 2011
Badgley Publishing Company
All rights reserved

Contents

Three accounts of the Battle of Buffington Island ------------------------ 5

From the Journal of Private Curtis R. Burke
Company B, 14th Regiment, Kentucky Cavalry, CSA ----------------- 43

Statement from Colonel Basil W. Duke
2nd Kentucky Cavalry, CSA -- 55

Notes, Telegrams, Statements and Facts ------------------------------ 65

The Fighting McCooks --- 83

The Deaths of Pulliam Halliday Hysell and Dr. William Hudson ----- 85

Statement of Interest by Steve Badgley --------------------------------- 87

The First Raider --- 91

Pictures of Interest --- 93

Three Accounts of the Battle of Buffington Island

Taken from *"The Rebellion Record, A Diary of American Events"* by Frank Moore. First published in 1864.

First Account

The uniform peace which sat brooding with dove-like wings over the State of the "Beautiful River" was broken for the first time during the threatened invasion under Bragg; but fate reserved for a rebel of far less military caliber and importance the remarkable event of bringing about and causing the first battle of the war in Ohio, and the first in her history as a State. But the sensation of the State is over, and the great Morgan raid is over forever.

The long, tedious, and perplexing pursuit of Morgan has ended at last in a victory such as will not only add lustre to our land and naval forces engaged, but render famous the scene of his defeat, which is, without doubt, the deathblow to the brilliant career of the notorious and wonderfully successful guerrilla chief. The local press of the State has chronicled from time to time the progress of the rebel force toward the point where it was met and defeated, and it only now remains to recount in a necessarily general manner.

Buffington Island lies in the Ohio River close to the Ohio shore, about thirty-five miles above Pomeroy, and was chosen by the rebels as a place of crossing into Virginia on account of the shoals between it and Blennerhasset's Island, twenty miles above. They had doubtless been well advised of the movements of our forces sent from all points, to either head them off or keep them confined to the only route eastward for them, until they reached the mountainous region and the eastern frontier. Without following, then, the progress of Morgan's march eastward, we will take a glance at his course previous to the morning of the battle. Yesterday, Sunday, the nineteenth, Morgan's right kept the main or shore road, from Pomeroy, having sent out skirmishers to feel the strength of that town and Middleport This was on Friday night, but if he had any intention to attempt to ford at Eight Mile Island, lie abandoned it on account of a show of resistance made by a small body of home guards, with a piece of ordnance made of cast-iron, and used only to fire salutes. A skirmish took place, in which the rebels lost two men killed and two or three wounded, and the home guards had one man slightly wounded and lost their gun, which, however, the rebels contemptuously left behind, after they found its utter uselessness. The main body was advancing on the road from Vinton, and uniting with the right, the entire force took the old stage-road to Pomeroy, and pushed for Buffington Island, or rather the shore opposite, which it reached, it is supposed, at two o'clock on Sunday morning.

When General Judah started from Portsmouth on Thursday evening, the sixteenth, it was expected that an engagement would take place; for reliable information had been received at the headquarters of Colonel P. Kinney, commander of the post, during the afternoon, that the rebels were at Miamiville, about eleven miles out. Now it was not the design to either court or bring on an engagement, as it was shown that the rebels were scattered over fifty or sixty miles of country, and the necessary concentration which they must make was rather humored than otherwise, so that the result would culminate in the complete capture or destruction of the entire horde.

General Judah then kept as close as possible to the rebels, but between them and the river, where that was practicable, until Morgan reached Jackson. Judah then pushed for Centerville, thinking that the enemy would take that route for the river; but he avoided it, and took through Winchester and Vinton toward Pomeroy, and thence north of that to the scene of action.

Our gunboats, namely, Moose, (flag-boat,) Reindeer, Springfield, Naumkeag, and Victory, in command of Lieutenant Commander Le Roy Fitch, were patrolling the river from an accessible point below Ripley to Portsmouth; but as soon as it was definitely ascertained that Morgan was pushing eastward, the Moose, towed by the Imperial, started up-stream, followed at proper distances by the other boats. The Moose made the foot of Buffington Island on Saturday night, and remained until next morning, without changing position, on account of a dense fog.

The rebel force made the shore opposite and above the island, as before stated, at two o'clock, and took position, under cover of artillery, in an extensive corn and wheat-field, skirted by hills and woods on its north and east sides. The position was a good one, and might have been hold to advantage for a much longer time than it was, but for the cooperation of the gunboat Moose, the only one of the fleet which arrived in time to participate in the fight.

The rebels had their artillery placed on the highest elevation on the east and completely commanded the Pomeroy road, over which General Judah's force, heretofore enumerated by your correspondent, came filing along unaware of the close proximity of the enemy. It should be noted here that the old stage-road to Pomeroy, over which Morgan came, and the lower road travelled by Judah, meet in an acute angle three quarters of a mile from the battlefield. Our column came along the lower road within range at six o'clock, having marched all night, having started from Pomeroy, and was not as fresh by five or six hours' rest as the enemy.

The rebels met us in solid column, and moved in battalions, and at the first fire repulsed our advance, which was too far ahead to be assisted by our artillery. This was the best opportunity they had to make a successful fight, but we fell back to bring forward our artillery, and the enemy did not seem to care to follow up the advantage. During this encounter Captain John J. Grafton, of General Judah's staff, became separated from the advance and narrowly escaped capture, by shooting, as he represents, the rebel cavalryman who seized him. He was dismounted, and being left on the ground made his way with considerable difficulty to the river, where he hailed the Moose and got aboard. Meantime the fight progressed, but in a desultory manner, until our artillery got into position and our lines were drawn closely around the enemy. A furious onset was made on our side and the rebels were driven over the field eastward and sought the shelter of the woods beyond.

No more fortunate circumstance could have transpired for the Union force than the escape of Captain Grafton to the gunboat Moose, for he pointed out to Lieutenant Commander Fitch the exact position of the rebels, and enabled that officer to so direct his guns as to throw shell in their very midst. The Moose is armed with twenty four pounder Dahlgren guns, the most accurate and effective gun in the service for operation against exposed bodies of men, and on this occasion the weapon did not belie its character. A dense fog, however, prevailed, which prevented Lieutenant Fitch doing as great execution in the rebel works as he desired, but his shots from the larboard and forward guns told, and an extensive scattering took place. The Moose opened at seven o'clock, and as the rebels were driven she kept steadily moving up-stream, throwing shell and shrapnel over the heads of our lads into the ranks of the enemy.

It now became evident that the rebels were being pressed in all directions, and that hard fighting would not save them from destruction.

A simultaneous rush was then made for the river, and throwing away arms and even clothing, a large body ran down to the shore, some with horses and some without, and plunged into the stream. The point chosen to effect the crossing was one mile and a half above the head of Buffington Island, and the movement would undoubtedly have been attended with considerable success but for the presence and performance of the gunboat. The crossing was covered by a twenty-pounder Parrott and a twelve-pound howitzer dragged into position by the rebels in their hasty retreat, but before the guns could be loaded and sighted the bow guns of the Moose opened on the rebel guns and drove the gunners away, after which the pieces were captured. Some twenty or thirty men only succeeded in crossing into Virginia at this point. Several were killed in the water, and many returned to the shore. While this was transpiring on the river, the roar of battle was still raging on the shore and back into the country. Basil Duke, under whoso generalship the fight was conducted, was evidently getting the worst of it, and his wearied gangs of horse-thieves, cut-throats, and non-descripts began to bethink them only of escape. Many threw down their arms, were taken prisoners and sent to the rear. Others sought the shelter of trees, or ran wildly from one point to another, and thus exposed themselves far more to the deadly chances of the field than if they had displayed courage and stood up to the fight.

A running fight next ensued, as the main force of the enemy retreated upstream toward a point on the Ohio shore, opposite Belleville, Va. The retreat was made as rapidly as possible, but considerable confusion was apparent. The gunboat kept almost ahead of the retreating column, and, when practicable, threw shells over the river bank toward it. It is said that the retreat was headed by Morgan, for Basil Duke was taken prisoner in the early part of the fight, but it was as rapidly followed up as possible. The Moose reached Belleville in time to fire upon the first party that attempted to cross the river. The crew report eight or nine killed and several wounded in the water, but twenty rebels or more got safely ashore in Virginia. It should have been stated above that General Scammon, with reinforcements from the Kanawha, arrived at the first scene of action in time to participate, but instead of landing his men on the Ohio side he disembarked them on the Virginia shore. This precaution may have been well enough in the event of the enemy effecting a crossing, but when the Moose moved up General Scammon re-embarked his troops, and went up with the gunboat to head off Morgan's retreat.

Foiled at Belleville, the rebels still kept pushing up along the shore, and again attempted to cross at Hawkinsport,(Hockingport) fourteen miles above the island, but again their efforts proved abortive on account of the gunboat.. Passing Hawkinsport,(Hockingport) the Moose came to Lee's Creek, Va., where she was greeted by a sharp volley of rifles and musketry from an ambuscade on the shore. It was now the turn of the starboard gunners to try the temper of their metal, and a smashing broadside was poured into the sneaking rascals on the "sacred soil." It was sufficient, for not another shot was fired, and Lieutenant Fitch learned afterward that nine of the bushwhackers were killed and several wounded.

The transports containing General Scammon's forces were then run up to a point between Hawkinsport, (Hockingport) Ohio, and Lee's Creek, Va., and landed on the Ohio shore, to intercept the rebel retreat. This is the last information we had on the river of that expedition, although it was reported in the evening that Scammon had captured the force or compelled it to surrender.

While the Moose was winning her laurels the other boats of the fleet were not failing to enact their regularly assigned part of the programme, which was to guard the fords below the island, and prevent any skulking squads of the rebels crossing to the much wished for Virginia shore. It is said that some of Morgan's men sang, "Oh! Carry me back to ole Virginny," with a pathos and sincerity of tone quite suggestive, not to say touching, and it certainly cannot be denied that Captain Fitch "went for them" with a degree of alacrity which proved his entire willingness to assist them as far as he could. The only regret which now in any way disturbs the repose of this officer is, that the rebels did not make a larger draft on the Moose, which might have been used as a ferryboat to carry them even farther on their *direct* road than they bargained for. As it was, she did all she could under the circumstances, and as the river was falling very fast, she, together with the others comprising the fleet, was compelled to return downstream. The Alleghany Belle, a light draught boat was fitted up temporarily for the occasion and armed with a rifled gun protected with bales of cotton, to guard the fords between Belleville and Buffington Island.

Tho scene of the battle was one of the most composite, perhaps, in the panorama of the war. The rebels were dressed in every possible manner peculiar to civilized man, but, generally speaking, their attire was very good. They wore in many instances large slouch hats peculiar to the slave States, and had their pantaloons stuck in their boots. A dirty, gray-colored coat was the most prevalent, although white "dusters" were to be seen.

They were armed with carbines, Enfield rifles, sabers, and revolvers, were well mounted, and looked in good health although jaded and tired. The battlefield and the roads surrounding it were strewn with a thousand articles never seen perhaps on a battlefield before. One is accustomed to see broken swords, muskets, and bayonets, haversacks, cartridge boxes, belts, pistols, gun-carriages, caissons, cannon, wagons upset, wounded, dead, and dying on the battlefield, but besides all these on the battlefield of Buffington Island, one could pick up almost any article in the dry goods, hardware, house-furnishing, or ladies' or gentlemen's furnishing line. Hats, boots, gloves, knives, forks, spoons, calico, ribbons, drinking cups, buggies, carriages, market wagons, circus wagons, and an almost endless variety of articles useful and all more or less valuable. An inventory of Morgan's plunder would tax the patience of an auctioneer's clerk, and I question if one man's life would be long enough to minutely catalogue the articles picked up during his raid.

The carnage of the field was not remarkable, although little groups of rebels were found slain by the deadly fragments of shell.

The result, as far as heard from at this time is all that could be wished for by the country. The entire rebel force was met; engaged, defeated, routed, and partially captured. All the enemy's arms, guns, accoutrements, most of his horses and all his plunder, were taken or fell into our hands, but the "full particulars" of his defeat and capture must be made the subject of another communication.

Nearly one thousand seven hundred prisoners are now in our hands, under guard of the Eighth Michigan Cavalry, and others are constantly arriving by our scouts and pursuing parties.

Prisoners admit a loss of two hundred killed and wounded on the field, while our loss will not exceed a fourth of that number. The rebel raid into the North is over. It has been destroyed, and the prestige of its notorious leader is gone.

The saddest incident of the fight is the wounding of Major McCook, father of the lamented Colonel McCook, murdered last summer by guerrillas in Kentucky. The old gentleman received a shot in the breast, which is represented as very serious, but it is to be hoped that it may not prove so. Major McCook is a patriotic, loyal, sturdy old gentleman, who clung to the service for his country's sake, and especially because he desired above all things to assist in ridding it of an armed tyranny and despotism under which such a mode of warfare prospers as left him to lament the untimely death of a brave and loyal son.

From papers found in the chests of the enemy's artillery, it would appear that Byrne's Battery, Captain John McMurray, First Kentucky Brigade, was the one used by Morgan, besides two twenty-pound Parrotts, which, after all, he had the energy and foresight to drag over the country in his remarkable march. One of these Parrotts and a brass piece were captured by Lieutenant Commander Fitch; all the other guns, five or six in number, were captured by the army.

The home guard and militia companies in the immediate neighborhood of the battlefield, and indeed along the lines of march, contributed very largely to the result, and were mainly instrumental in preventing the rebels from striking at points where a great destruction of property would necessarily have followed.

At Middleport the militia captured several prisoners; at Syracuse, eighty-five were brought in; at Racine, seventy-eight. Skirmishes frequently occurred between the rebel scouts and small parties of armed citizens, and many a household will have reason to remember the Morgan raid. But more than a score of rebels "bit the dust" during the last two or three days of the raid, and were laid low by the unerring aim of the sturdy farmer of Southwestern (Southeastern!)Ohio, so suddenly called to the defense of his home and happy fireside.

The loyal women of Portsmouth, Pomeroy, and other towns and villages, were not wanting in thoughtfulness for our brave boys on their perplexing and hurried marches. They prepared food and had it ready at all times, day and night, and with ready hands and smiling faces supplied the wants of the "brave defenders of our country." Nothing so gladdens the heart of the soldier as the kindly attention of patriotic women, for with the memory of their goodness and sweetness in his heart he goes forth encouraged to continued deeds of valor, which shall make their common future more peaceful and secure.

One of the features of the pursuit and defeat of the rebels was the wonderful stories of John Morgan and his conduct through Ohio. Some had it that he was "a perfect gentleman"—that most vulgar of phrases to express one of the greatest rarities on the face of the earth; while others were ready to swear that he had committed all the crimes known to the code, prominent among which were murder, rape, arson, and highway robbery. It would prove a bootless task to sift these stories, and a mere imposition upon the credulity and time of the reader to recount them. They are in no way relevant to the purpose of the present writing, and, if for no other reason, are left untold.

The rebels took one of our guns at the first charge, and captured over twenty prisoners, but these they immediately paroled, and the gun they never used, for it was soon recovered, with the capture of all their own.

In closing this general account of the last moments of the Morgan raid, which culminated in the battle of Buffington Island, a name I have given it because no other place of note lay near the scene, 1 have to express my regret at not being able to speak intelligently of the operation of General Hobson, and in fact of all the forces engaged, besides those of General Judah, General Scammon, and the gunboat Moose. Time was pressing and opportunities limited, but the best use was made of them.

The gratitude of the country is due our soldiers and sailors to whose efforts the successful result of the brief but perplexing campaign against Morgan is due, and I know I hazard nothing in bespeaking for them the lasting gratitude of the patriotic and loyal people of Ohio.   E. B

2nd Account

Cincinnati, July 23, 1868.

Mr. Editor:

Upon the invitation of General Judah I applied to General Cox for permission to accompany him on his late expedition after John Morgan and Co., as Vol. A. D. C, which was kindly granted. We left this city Wednesday, the fifteenth, with about one thousand two hundred cavalry and artillery, arriving at Portsmouth the following afternoon, immediately disembarking, and at nine o'clock in the evening started in pursuit toward Oak Hill or Portland. During the night the guide lost his way, which caused us to march several miles more than we liked. At early day we arrived at Webster and halted an hour, after which we started for Oak Hill, at which place we learned that the rapid wild rangers were at Jackson destroying property and were about going eastward. General Judah immediately started for Centreville, a point on the main road to Gallipolis, some six miles distant, to intercept the villains. General Manson was sent for from Portsmouth, who was awaiting orders with a good infantry force to cooperate when he might with advantage. Judah arrived, after a hasty march of less than two hours, and took possession of the town for the night, making such disposition of his forces that all were anxious to have Morgan come that way to the river and try his disposition for a fight, but he took the old road from Jackson to Pomeroy, through Vinton, while we started early next morning for the same place through Potter. We arrived at Pomeroy about four o'clock, a few hours after Morgan had been scared away by a slight fight with the home guards and the close proximity of the United States forces under General Scammon. The roads to Pomeroy had been by the people barricaded very effectually to prevent the murderers from entering without trouble their active and thriving little city.

After a few hours' rest the order was sounded at ten o'clock at night to advance, which was obeyed with eager desire to go ahead, for all felt that General Judah knew his business, although he was suffering from severe illness known only by his surgeons, Dr. Kimberly of his staff, and Hunt of Covington, a personal friend. Some wiseacres at Pomeroy attempted to induce the General to follow Morgan *via* Chester, which would have increased our distance to Buffington some ten miles, but he, Napoleon-like, heard all reasonable suggestions and then decided promptly to go through Racine, which was his own judgment, and not thought well of by some who assumed to "know it all." After a tiresome night-march, day dawned, and within a few miles of the river rumors reached us that the enemy had crossed during the night. We pressed on. A scouting party returned from the river saying all was clear on our road. A paroled home guard and an escaped negro corroborated each other in saying that Morgan was now over the river, as they had been with him a few hours before, and it was his intention then to "push right on." We were then only a mile from the bar, and the General urging up the rear with the artillery, pushed forward with the Michigan Cavalry in advance, himself, staff, and escort following close behind. A dense fog covered all the bottom lands so that we moved slowly forward. About half a mile from the river Captain W. H. Day and Dr. J. F. Kimberly saw upon the left, the enemy in line of battle, not seventy yards from us. It was doubted at first, but in a moment the whistling minie, carbine and pistol-balls were sending loud and quick calls for us to halt. Our road being narrow, and we confined by strong fences, with ditches on either side of us, all that was left for us was to retreat as best we could a few rods. Here it was that the noble and brave old hero, Major Daniel McCook, received his two mortal wounds, of which he died on Tuesday, twenty-first, on the boat from Portland to Pomeroy. Upon our retreat Captains R. C. Kise, A. A.G., ___ Grafton, Vol. A. D. C, and Henshaw, of said battery, were, with a number of others, taken prisoners, and one piece of artillery captured. Lieutenant F. G. Price, a gallant young officer of the staff, was also seriously wounded in the head, which disabled him for the rest of the day.

For a time our prospects were quite dark, the fog was over us, the enemy near, and we entire strangers as to their localities, but Providence was with those who were for the Republic. The fog suddenly lifted, and the General, with Captains Day and J. E. McGowan, and Lieutenant H. T. Bissell, were all gallantly and coolly giving orders and making ready for a good fight with the enemy, who now appeared from three to four thousand strong, immediately before us on the plains. Lieutenant O'Neil, of the Fifth Indiana cavalry, now appeared by another road with but fifty men, and charged two different regiments so desperately that they broke and left our captured gun, officers and men in our possession. The tide had turned. Our guns were soon in position, and in two hours the enemy had left the field in confusion, and were hastened in their movements by a gun of a Michigan battery on board the steamer Alleghany Belle, commanded by Captain Sebastian, and the gunboat Moose, commanded by Captain Fitch, U. S. N. Morgan's forces in their retreat soon fell into the hands of the noble Hobson, who had so persistently chased him for over four weeks, and then the rivalry, among our forces as to whom should gobble the most of the renegades commenced. General Shackleford and Colonel Woolford, with the Forty-fifth Ohio, all did good service, and helped to secure the prize, which could not have been done by either command alone. Immediately after a few hours' rest all the forces were sent in different directions by Generals Judah and Hobson to intercept the enemy. All the artillery Morgan had on the field, some five pieces, were taken by us. The spoils with which the trails of the runaways were littered would make an honest warrior blush to name, such as books, stationery, cutlery, dry goods of all descriptions, crockery, boots and shoes, hats and caps, women's wearing apparel of all names — some articles not to be mentioned—even old women's bonnets, to say nothing of carriages, harness, small arms of all kinds, and worn and jaded horses and mules by the hundred that are worth only the price of dead animals for the use of tallow-chandlers.

On the persons of most of the Rebels could be found greenbacks in abundance. Their own trash, which Brownlow says "is not worth ten cents a bushel," was also profuse among them. Watches and all kinds of jewelry, to a great extent, were in their pockets, which were not with them when they entered the North. The inference is that they are a band of robbers under the guise of an army.

General Judah, for a few days, will make Pomeroy his headquarters, as he is the ranking officer in that part of the country. It is thought that some of Hobson's and Judah's forces will yet trap John and his few retainers before they can reach Dixie.

A disgraceful coward, called Sontag, from Portsmouth with nearly four hundred men, well armed, surrendered to Morgan on Tuesday last without firing a gun. Morgan was in his grasp, if he had fought. Shame on such mountebanks! May he live long enough for his name to be a stench to himself, as it is to all who know him now.

I must not forget to testify to the intense loyal feeling manifested all along the route our army took. Many said Vallandigham's admirers were not as numerous as in days past. The raid may do good toward opening the eyes of the careless. May we not hope so?

It is again seen that the enemy attacked us on Sunday, and we whipped them. I only notice the fact Major McCook was wounded within a short time after the first repulse, recovered by Captain Day, and by him sent to the nearest house, where Dr. Kimberly gave him all the attention possible; but from the first, all hope of recovery was dispelled by the Major and the Doctor. His wounds were necessarily mortal. The enemy, while he was yet in their lines, robbed him of money, watch, and all loose articles on his person. The silvery locks of the patriot-hero were no protection against the "Kentucky gentlemen" of John Morgan's and Basil Duke's command. Captain Kise, and all of our men whom they held for a few minutes, were robbed of money and personal property. A pistol was placed at Captain Kise's head and his boots demanded, but an officer interfered, and the contemplated outrage was prevented. Pretty return for Grant's kindness, was it not!

Our loss is very light. All told, it will not exceed thirty killed and wounded—some five killed—at the outside. The enemy has thus far lost full two hundred killed and wounded, and not less than two thousand two hundred prisoners—among them about a hundred officers, including Colonels Basil Duke, Dick Morgan, Ward, Hoffman, and Smith. Considering how slight our loss was, it is the greatest victory of the war, and makes Judah and Hobson rightly entitled to two stars. Judah received his military education at West Point, and is a soldier in every respect. While he is not an abolitionist, there is no one who hates rebels more than he, or who is more willing to use all means (including the negro) to crush the rebellion—yea, even to the extermination of every rebel in the South, so that the desired end be accomplished. Hobson is a lawyer and a good soldier, having entered the service because he hated rebels and loved the old flag. The people will ever sing praise to Judah and Hobson.

Cincinnati was well represented in the chase by the gallant Guthrie Grays, commanded by Captain Disney, who ascended the river on the steamer Magnolia, and at the battle of Buffington Bar, were on the steamer Alleghany Belle, panting for a chance to return the fire on shore, while they were compelled to receive it from the enemy. They did good and valuable service as guard to the prisoners brought from Pomeroy on the steamer Ingomar. Of this company the Queen City may feel proud. May all the new Seventh prove as ready and effective as this tenth part have already. Success to the Seventh!

Nat Pepper, son of Captain Pepper, of the late steamer Alice Dean, was a volunteer private at the gun on the steamer Alleghany Belle, which the rebels say did the most execution of any of our artillery. He is an only son, about eighteen years of age, and is anxious to remain in the service. Would that many who are older had the same willingness to risk their lives for the Republic.

Captain Wood, of the Eighteenth regulars, while stationed at Marietta, as mustering officer, was induced to take command of two companies of volunteers and proceeded to Buffington Bar on Saturday. He found the steamer Starlight aground, with only two men aboard, and loaded with three thousand barrels of flour. He immediately unloaded the vessel, raised steam and manned the boat, from the captain to the dock-hand, with his men, and run her out of the range of Morgan's guns, which, before he could get away, had arrived on the bank. Before leaving with his little band of true gallants, he rolled his two heavy pieces of artillery over into a ravine, so that the enemy could neither take nor use them. After the fight Captain Wood reported to General Judah for duty, with the boat, and was highly complimented by the General, and placed in charge of several hundred of the prisoners to bring to Cincinnati. Had the boat not been seized by Captain Wood when it was, Morgan would have had it, and crossed the river with it; for the gunboats did not arrive till Sunday morning, while Morgan was there the night before; so let Marietta be proud of her gentlemen soldiers, who were not too proud to carry coal or do any work which would hinder the enemies of the Union and help her defenders.

The South boasts that all of her people are in the fight — rich and poor, old and young — and that they can yet whip us. When all our rich and poor and old and young, who are at heart right, are engaged, we can whip the South, even if France and England do help them. Our people have not yet awakened out of sleep. Only a little more of this kind of work from Wood and Vallandigham's friends, and the honest people, who are for the Union without an if or but, will arise and overthrow all who oppose them, to the eternal shame of all traitors. G. P. E.

3rd Account

On the twenty-seventh of June, 1863, the Second and Seventh Ohio cavalry and the Forty-fifth Ohio mounted infantry, together with Laws' howitzer battery, left Somerset, Ky., for Jamestown, for the purpose of watching Morgan, who, with his whole brigade, was encamped on the other side of the Cumberland River. We lay there from the twenty-ninth June to the third July; more or less skirmishing going on all the while—when on that day Captain Carter of the First Kentucky Cavalry, with detachments of the Second Ohio cavalry and Forty-fifth Ohio Mounted Infantry, went on a reconnaissance toward Columbia. There they had a fight with the advance of Morgan's division, which we then found had crossed the river on the second of July. About five o'clock on the afternoon of the third, Captain Carter was very seriously wounded, and the enemy pressed us so closely, that we were compelled to fall back. At six o'clock a detachment of the First Kentucky, Seventh Ohio cavalry, and Forty-fifth Ohio mounted infantry left Jamestown to reinforce Carter, and arrived at Columbia about eleven o'clock. They found Carter in a dying condition, and Morgan with three brigades in full possession of the town.

A short struggle ensued between us, for we had not then learned the strength of the enemy, and supposed it to be a force we might easily crush; but as the fight went on we found the forces with which we were contending were larger than we had supposed; when we fired musketry we were answered with grape and canister; when we fired a few rifle shots we were answered with whole volleys of musketry; and speedily beating a hasty retreat, we went as fast as our horses would carry us to Jamestown. We reached that place about five o'clock on the morning of the fourth, and a courier was instantly dispatched by Colonel Wolford to General Carter, in command of the United States forces at Somerset, announcing that Morgan, with his whole force, had effected a crossing of the Cumberland River at Burkesville, and had advanced north to Columbia. From this date the pursuit of Morgan commenced.

At six o'clock P.m. there was an unusual amount of satisfaction expressed in the countenances of our boys, for orders had just been issued for all the mounted troops stationed in Jamestown to prepare to move at a moment's notice, and to provide themselves with six days' rations. It was a relief after the wearisome monotony incidental to the comparative inactivity of camp life, to be suddenly called into active service, and, if I must admit it—the pleasure was none the less, because the prospects were that the chase would not be too long to be pleasant. Our boys therefore set about making their preparations with a will, and in a few moments we were ready to start. It was well that there was so much alacrity displayed, for these first orders were barely issued before it was followed by another ordering us off at once, and a few moments more saw us fairly off in pursuit of the celebrated raider.

We could not have made a more propitious start. The night was fine, clear and cool. The moon, although occasionally obscured by light fleecy clouds, gave sufficient light to enable us to see well and clearly all around us, so that we were to some extent free from apprehensions of a sudden attack from any hidden foe. The weather was sufficiently cool to enable us to ride along without discomfort, and altogether the ride from Jamestown to the banks of the Green River, on that splendid July night, was one of the pleasantest marches our boys have ever made. Tho future we cared little about; chatting and laughing and singing, we proceeded gaily enough on our journey, occasionally speculating among ourselves where we should meet with the man who had become the great object of our desires, and what we should do with him when we got him, for the possibility of his escaping from us was never entertained for a moment.

We reached the northern bank of the Green River about daylight on Sunday morning, the fifth instant, and after a hurried breakfast we again started in pursuit, marching all that day and camping on Sunday night, at eight o'clock, at Casey street, where we were joined by the Second Tennessee mounted infantry. The result of our observations convinced us that our commissary department had been neglected. We had been ordered to prepare ourselves with six days' rations, but many of our boys, having faith in Providence, had failed to provide themselves, and the consequence was, we found ourselves with a bare average of three days' rations for the whole number of troops. Consoling ourselves with vague speculations as to the prospects for foraging, we lay down to rest that night, and started again in pursuit at half-past six o'clock the next morning, the sixth instant, and drew rein again at Bradfordsville at ten o'clock. There we heard, for the first time since our departure, of any of the movements of Morgan. We were informed that he had captured our forces at Lebanon, and had then left that place for Bargetown. Leaving Bradfordsville within half an hour of our arrival, we took up our line of march for

Lebanon, arriving there at three o'clock in the afternoon. At this place our forces had made some resistance, in which Tom Morgan, the brother of the guerrilla chieftain, was killed. In revenge the rebels burned some eighteen or twenty houses, robbed the post-office, cleaned out the stores, and plundered and robbed and destroyed all they could lay their hands on. An incident occurred here which may perhaps be worth relating. An old man living in Lebanon had two sons in Morgan's command, who had been with him ever since the commencement of his military career. During the absence of the young men, the old man's house and lot had been sold at sheriff's sale, and had been purchased by a strong Union man.

The rebels were informed of all these circumstances by the two sons, and proceeding to the house they burnt it to the ground, leaving its owner almost penniless to begin the world again. Another significant thing began to be evident here. John Morgan, who had heretofore been so popular with all Kentucky men, was beginning to lose a little of his popularity. Certain little murmurs, of discontent reached our ears for the first time from some of those who are spoken of by the out-and-out traitors—as "good, strong Kentuckians." Morgan's men, in their passage through the central part of the State, had been blinded to some extent by the superior refulgence of" State rights," and had, in a great measure, lost sight of individual rights. And many were the complaints of those who once possessed property which was not forthcoming, and who refused to be comforted by the reflection that it was all for the good of the sunny South.

Leaving Lebanon at half-past three, we arrived at Springfield at six o'clock, and there we met many of those belonging to the Union forces which had been captured by the rebels at Lebanon.

These men presented a very sorry appearance when we arrived among them. The number of troops captured by the rebels at Lebanon was about three hundred. Immediately on surrendering, the rebels had made them fall in, and putting a guard around them had forced them to march on foot at a double-quick from Lebanon to Springfield—a distance of fully twelve miles. During the way many of them exhibited signs of giving out, but they were compelled to keep up by their merciless captors. At last one sergeant found it impossible to keep up with the ranks. The guards knocked him down with the butt end of their muskets, and his brains were tramped out by the feet of the horses of the rebel rearguard, and his body left lying in the road. On their arrival at Springfield they were paroled, the Southern chivalry first robbing them of every dollar they had.

We camped on the night of the sixth at eight o'clock, on the Bargetown Road, about six miles beyond Springfield, and left again the next morning at two o'clock, reaching Bargetown at six. Here we found that Morgan had left that place at noon on the day before, going north on the Shepherdsville road. We were joined at this place by General Hobson, with Shackleford's brigade, comprising the Third, Eighth, Ninth, and Twelfth Kentucky cavalry and two pieces of artillery. General Hobson now took command and continuing our journey we encamped on the night of the seventh about four miles from Shepherdsville. It was at this point that Morgan captured the mail-train on the Louisville and Nashville Railroad, and had captured and paroled about, twenty soldiers who were passengers on board the cars. They also robbed all the passengers of any valuables they might have about them, stole all the contents of the mail-bags and appropriated all the express packages that were on board. Here our horses began to give out We had been in the saddle with hardly any rest since the evening of the fourth of July, and it was more than horse-flesh could endure, so to recruit our horses we went into camp at six o'clock in the evening. On the morning of the eighth we were again on our way at half-past four o'clock, General Shackleford's brigade in the advance, and crossed the railroad where the rebels had robbed the mail. They had taken all the letters with them to amuse themselves by reading as they went along, and for twenty-five or thirty miles the road was strewed with fragments of paper—the letters which the rebels had thrown down in the way to become the sport of every breath of air that blew, or to be picked up by any passer-by who might chance to come along. As we followed along the road we curiously picked up many of the notes and letters which were scattered so profusely around, and attempted to decipher the writing, an undertaking attended with considerable difficulty, for the writing—not often too distinct—was rendered almost totally illegible by reason of dust and dirt and the trampling of horses' feet. The first we picked out of the mass of fluttering paper commenced with "My dear wife," and, after a few commonplace remarks, went on to speak of some crushing trial that had lately fallen upon them both in the death of a loved relative, while the writer attempts to impart comfort in the affliction, and to lighten the load of grief, which, he says, he fears is greater than she can bear. The next is altogether different in character. It is a business letter and says: "Enclosed please find one hundred and fifty dollars, which you will please place to my credit". A third is written in rather a clerical sort of handwriting—at least it appears so to us. It commences very formally with "Madame," and in it we find that it has become the painful duty of the writer to inform her for whom the letter is intended that her husband "is no more." That after lingering for many weeks in some hospital, he had quietly breathed his last, with his last breath sending a message to the only woman he loved on earth. The letter covers all the four sides of the paper, but a large part is torn off, and singularly enough we cannot find a single name to give us any clue either to the parties to whom it was addressed, or to the writer of the sad news. A fourth letter is full of hope and joy, and speaks of weddings and dances and balls in a strange sort of jumbled-up way; while another is very sad, and gives a long description of a death-bed scene or a funeral. So they go on, strangely like the ever-changing scenes of every-day life, one day dark and cloudy, and the next light and cheerful, and so amusing ourselves with perusing the letters, and reflecting on their contents, the day's march is made. Quietly enough, for the letters seem to have set every one thinking what will be the result of the loss of news. Thinking of children waiting to hear from a parent away off in the armies of the Tennessee, of a sister watching for news of a dear brother, of the news of the death of a husband to a newly-made widow and speculating as to whether the news will ever reach her. So we go on to Lawrenceville, about one mile from which place we pass the night. A little tiny stream runs close by our encampment, and I stroll out in the night and throw myself down by its side, and gaze on the little ripples that seem to glide over its surface. It was flowing on so peacefully and calmly in the midst of our warlike movements that I insensibly catch myself repeating part of Willis's description of the pursuit of King David by his son Absalom, and saying:

"Now strikingly the course of nature tells, by Its light heed of human suffering, that it was fashioned for a happier world."

But, as I get so far, I suddenly find I have company, and am joined by one of my comrades, who, having hoard my involuntary soliloquy, accuses me of getting sentimental, and shaking off the spell that seemed to enthrall me, I return to camp, and throwing myself on the ground, I sleep soundly until morning breaks, and the bugle calls us once more to mount.

Here we are informed that Morgan left Elizabethtown on his right, and struck for Brandenburg, commencing to cross the Ohio River on the Alice Dean and the J. T. McCoombs. On the morning of the ninth, we again started in pursuit, feeling a little elated to find that we have gained something on him in the journey. We captured three prisoners shortly after leaving Lawrenceville, who told us that at the fight at Green River they lost one hundred and ten men in killed and wounded, including Colonel Chenault, one major and four captains. . As we drew near to Brandenburg we saw a thick smoke rising up from the river, and quickened our speed in hopes of arriving in time to prevent the destruction of property which we presumed was going on, but as we arrived in the town we could see down in the river the Alice Dean burning rapidly away on the other side of the stream, while far back on the opposite shore of the river, could be seen the rear-guard of Morgan's force rapidly disappearing in the distance. The complaints of the inhabitants were longer, and deeper, and louder than at any other point on our route. The accustomed chivalry of Morgan's men, which is a matter of so much pride and exultation among the secesh of Kentucky, is, it seems, excelled by their cupidity, and they could not withstand the temptation offered by the well filled stores of Brandenburg. Plundering all indiscriminately, there was hardly a house in the place which had not suffered more or less from their visit. One firm, that of Weatherspool and Joekel, they robbed of goods to the amount of three thousand five hundred dollars, and when they expostulated with them for taking such goods as could not possibly be of service to them, such as silks and muslins, they replied that they wanted them to present to their Yankee cousins in Indiana.

In the fight that took place at Brandenburg, at the time of the crossing, between the Leavenworth home guards and Morgan's men, they killed two of the Indianans and took forty-five of them prisoners, capturing their twelve pounder gun, which they threw into the river after spiking it In the onward march of the rebels they burnt Peter Locke's mill, which lies about three miles from the river. This was the first work of destruction they performed after they commenced to invade the Free States.

Our forces commenced to cross the river at noon of the ninth of July, and went into camp on the hill opposite Brandenburg until the whole force was across, in order to give our horses rest, that they might be fresh when they resumed the pursuit At three o'clock on the morning of the tenth, all our forces were across, and breaking up our camp, we at once resumed the pursuit About five miles on the road we captured Lieutenant Arnold, of Gano's Regiment, who was thrown from his horse and sprained his ankle, thus being rendered unfit for duty. Arriving at Corydon at ten o'clock we found that the home guards had made a stand there under Colonel Timberley, and had fought them for four hours, killing two of Morgan's men, and wounding seven, while they themselves lost fifteen in killed and wounded. It was at this place that Mr. Glenn was shot down, and his house burnt for having fired on the rebels as they passed by his house. As we rode by the place, the dead body of Robinson, the rebel he had killed, was still laid out in the open air, waiting for its burial to take place. In Corydon we found that here, as everywhere else, they had cleaned out all the stores, and had plundered all they could lay their hands on. Three mills which are situated in this place they threatened to burn, unless they raised one thousand dollars each in fifteen minutes. The money was raised and the mills were saved.

They captured two hundred home guards and paroled them, and when they left, they took with them all the horses they could find, Dick Morgan's regiment taking the advance. Up to this time they had stolen altogether about two hundred and fifty horses and had torn up and destroyed all the American flags they could find.

Encamping that night about two and a half miles from Salem, we broke camp at five o'clock on the eleventh, and arrived there quite early in the morning. We met with quite a grand reception there, the inhabitants supplying us with all the eatables we required, and doing for us all they had in their power. Morgan had burnt the railroad bridge across the Blue River at this point, and had also levied his usual tax of one thousand dollars each on the three mills of the place; and finished up by robbing all the houses in the place. At one or two houses, the inhabitants had locked up and fled at their approach, but they broke in the doors and helped themselves to all they could find.

On Saturday, July eleventh, we encamped at Vienna, where the rebels had burnt the bridge, and we found that Morgan had struck for Lexington and thence north; so leaving camp again at five o'clock on the morning of the twelfth, we followed on to Paris, where the rebels had made but a short stay, being apprehensive that we were too close in their rear for their own comfort At Vernon, Morgan sent in to Colonel Lowe, who commanded the one thousand two hundred militia who had assembled at that point, demanding a surrender. Colonel Lowe replied: "Come and take it." Morgan then notified him to remove all the women and children, which was done. He then surrounded the town, burnt the bridges, and did all the damage that lay in his power, and then went on to DuPont without troubling himself to fight, and there burnt the railroad bridge and two other bridges, and left for Versailles, where he robbed the county treasurer of five thousand dollars, all the money he had, and again took his departure, expressing his sincere regret that the county was so very poor.

We arrived at Versailles on the thirteenth, at five o'clock, and found that Morgan, after sacking the town, had sent on a force to Osgood, where they burnt a bridge and captured a telegraph operator, and kept on to Pierceville, burning all the bridges on the road, and starting thence to Milan. They then struck off on the Brookfield road, and after travelling eight miles, turned off toward Wisebergh, where they had a skirmish with the homo guards. At New Ulsas, a small German settlement, they captured a wagon-load of lager beer, which they carried with them to refresh themselves on their way. On the night of the thirteenth, we encamped at Harrison, our horses being thoroughly jaded and worn out, and men being in a condition not much more encouraging than their horses. On that night Morgan nearly surrounded Cincinnati. Starting at three A.m. on the fourteenth, we followed in the wake of Morgan's troops through Springdale and Sharon to Montgomery, where we found he had captured one hundred and fifty good horses. At Miamiville, after turning over the train on the Little Miami Railroad, he burnt fifty new Government wagons. There had been two hundred wagons, but we succeeded in saving one hundred and fifty, together with one thousand mules. We camped that night at nine o'clock at Camp Repose, and started at two A.m. op the fifteenth for Batavia. We were led out of our way by a Methodist preacher, who had undertaken to guide us, and so far succeeded in misleading us, that instead of going by the direct road, which was only six miles; he took us by a roundabout way of fifteen miles. Whether this was intentional or otherwise we did not know, but he seemed very anxious to make his escape, and if hard swearing on the part of our boys will injure anyone but the swearer, then is that Methodist preacher cursed for all eternity. Morgan on this day burnt two bridges on White Oak River, and Dick Morgan separated from the main body of the rebels with his regiment four miles from Williamsburgh and went to Georgetown, plundering that town. We encamped that night at Sardinia at eleven o'clock.

On the sixteenth instant, we broke camp at four o'clock in the morning and arrived at Winchester at eight. The rebels had entered the town at two p.m. of the previous day, had robbed the mail, and stolen thirty-five thousand dollars' worth of property and fifty horses. From one firm in this place they stole eleven thousand dollars' worth of property, which was the largest single robbery they effected during the whole of the raid. They tore up all the flags they could find at this place, and amused themselves by tying the fragments to mules' tails and driving them through the streets. At Jacktown they burnt a bridge and went on to Wheat Ridge, where they robbed an old man, who was hardly able to walk from old age and feebleness, of thirty dollars. Here their forces again separated; part going through Mount Olive. Six miles this side of Jackson the citizens blockaded the road, and detained Morgan two hours. With the exception of the fight by the home guards at Corydon, where the rebels were detained four hours, this was the best service rendered by citizens during the whole of the raid. At Jasper the rebels gave the proprietor twenty-five minutes to raise one thousand dollars, or they would burn his mill. He was unable to procure the money and the mill was burnt accordingly. We went into camp at Jasper at two a.m., on the seventeenth, and resumed our journey at eleven, having to swim our horses across the canal. One of our men, a member of company L, Second

Ohio, named McGoron, accidentally killed himself with his revolver. Arriving at Piketon we found that the rebels had killed a Mr. McDougal who was busily blockading the road when they came up. The same day they shot a Dr. Burroughs, who had fired on them as they passed by his place. We arrived at Jackson at six o'clock, where we were met with the same story we had heard so often before— robbery, and theft, and pillage, and destruction on every hand. There was one thing we must give the rebels credit for, and that is, that in the matter of thieving they showed the strictest impartiality, robbing the man who "had always been opposed to the war" with the same coolness with which they robbed his more loyal brethren. Indeed, it was with a kind of vindictive pleasure that they stole from those who were so forward in informing them that they had always been "good butternuts." At this place they destroyed the Jackson *Standard* printing-office — the only paper that they injured during the whole of the march. The home guards having reason to think it was done at the instigation of a butternut resident of the place, cleaned out the Jackson *Express* office, a copperhead sheet of the same place.

From this place Morgan had sent up some forces to Berlin, at which place there were three thousand militia posted, under the command of Colonel Runkle. Morgan's men threw one shell in their midst, which acted like a charm on the militia, who instantly became—missing.

We camped that night at Jackson, and started again at three o'clock on the morning of the eighteenth, and followed on by way of Keystone Furnace. We found that they had burnt a bridge over Raccoon Creek, and had captured two boxes of army clothing. At the little town of Linesville, the home guards tore up the bridge and blockaded the road, detaining the rebels another two hours, and doing as good service as the citizens of Jasper. Part of the rebel force had gone down by way of Wilkesville, where they burnt two or three bridges; we went on to Chester, where they had burnt a bridge over Shade Creek, and encamped for the night.

On the nineteenth, the battle of Buffington Island took place, if so slight a skirmish is worthy of the name of a battle. We started out at one o'clock, and at five o'clock we opened fire on the rear of the rebels, who were just then opening fire on General Judah's forces. The battle, although it has been often described, is not altogether well understood, on account of most correspondents having written from the gunboats and were of course unable to see much of the fight. The river road runs along nearly close to the bank of the river. About two miles back of the river, on the north side, runs a long range of hills, down over which comes a road running to the river at the island. About three hundred yards above this pike road was a small private roadway leading north into some corn-fields, while a large wheatfield separated the two roads from each other. The rebels had encamped on Saturday night in the cornfields at the end of the by-road or lane, and General Judah's men coming down on the pike road had come on them almost unawares, the density of the morning fog having obscured the rebels from their view. The rebels fired on the advancing column, throwing them into temporary disorder, and were preparing to make a charge, when the gunboats opened on them from the river, and at the same time the Second and Seventh Ohio, of

General Hobson's force, opened on them in their rear, having just come in a little way above the pike road, by which General Judah's forces had come up from Portsmouth. This staggered them for the time, and Colonel Saunders coming up immediately afterward with two pieces of artillery, threw two shells in their midst. Fired at from all sides, what could they do? Separating in two columns, one part of their force pushed forward to the right only to find themselves completely surrounded, and they quietly submitted themselves prisoners of war. Colonel Dick Morgan surrendered his command to General Shackleford, while Colonel Duke and Colonel Smith were cut off in a ravine, where they surrendered themselves to their captors. At this time the prisoners numbered about eight hundred and fifty. About forty-five men had succeeded in crossing over into Kentucky (West Virginia) before the fight commenced. A portion of the rebels, who ran to the left, at the end of the fight, numbering two hundred, marched under Colonel Johnston to Reedsville, where they succeeded in crossing over, with the loss of about twenty-five men who were killed by the fire of the gunboats. Another portion went up to Longgreen Bottom (Long Bottom), stealing all that lay in their way, crossing over at Harrisonville, and turning right around, struck for the river again, about forty miles below Buffington, where Coleman of Colonel Cluke's command surrendered all his force to about fifty men. The balance of Morgan's band accompanied their leader to Columbiana County, where they were all captured by General Shackleford.

So ends the great Morgan raid. It has proved one of the most remarkable events of the war, and God grant it may never be repeated.

From the Journal of Private Curtis R. Burke

Company B, 14th Regiment, Kentucky Cavalry, CSA

Curtis Rensellear Burke was born on January 24, 1842 in Massillon, Stark County, Ohio. His parents were Edward D. Burke and Anna Barbara Rice. The Burkes also lived in Mt. Vernon and Zanesville, Ohio, before moving to Kentucky around 1851. They lived in Frankfort, Maysville, and Lexington, Kentucky where Curtis Burke worked in his father's marble business.

Burke joined Captain John Hunt Morgan's company of Lexington Rifles, Kentucky State Guard, around 1860. On September 15, 1862, Burke mustered into "B" Company, 14th Regiment, Kentucky Cavalry (C.S.A.) as a private. His father Edward joined Murphy's Kentucky Calvary as a 1st Sergeant.

Burke served under John Hunt Morgan and participated in Morgan's Raid into Indiana and Ohio in July 1863. He was captured at Buffington Island, Ohio, and remained a prisoner of war at Camp Morton, Indianapolis, Indiana, and Camp Douglas, Chicago, Illinois until March 1865. He returned home to Lexington in June 1865. Burke died on November 5th, 1919.

Saturday, July 18th, 1863. Weather pleasant. We fed our horses well and saddled up. We moved early passing through the little village of D. where we saw a company of sappers and miners from our command with axes and shovels. The planks had been removed from the floor of a little bridge in the village by some home guards and hid so we had to go some distance to get by. We rode lively till about twelve o'clock when we came to a place in the road that was blockaded with trees cut across the road which brought us to a halt."

"We were within a few miles of Pomeroy, O. on the Ohio River where we intended going. The blockade was in a place where the road run between hills, besides it was defended by a strong force of home guards and bushwhackers to prevent our clearing away the obstructions. While we were waiting orders a lot of us went to a large white house on our right and got as much milk, bread, preserves, molasses, honey, etc. as we could eat and took some to the balance of the boys. The people had run off from home. Where people stayed at home and behaved themselves we did not disturb the house, but where people run away from home we rated them as home guards or bushwhackers, and took everything in the way of something to eat in the house. We waited about an hour and finding that we would lose too much time in clearing out the obstructions we turned back nearly a mile and took a road to our tight. The road was in a bottom or valley following the course of a branch [creek]. As usual the dust flew in clouds. We did not go far before the advance guard was stopped by a volley from home guards on a high bluff of rocks in a fork in the road. A ridge on our left sheltered us. We dismounted to fight. The enemy's firing sounded as if it was nearing the fence on top of the ridge. So we hurried up to get the fence first. On reaching the fence we were surprised to find a deep wide valley with the left fork of the road between us and the enemy. We were ordered not to waste our ammunition as they were too far off to do any execution. Their spent balls passed over us once in a while. We fired a shot a piece at them to get the old loads out and load fresh again. Co. C and D. with assistance of [Colonel Adam "Stovepipe"] Johnson's regiment dismounted and took up the hill on the right and flanked the party at the bluff driving them off. The right hand fork of the road led to the river but it was strongly blockaded. I could see the black clouds of smoke rising from the gunboats and transports on the other side of the hills in front of us. I was surprised to find that we were so close to the river. We mounted our horses and took the left fork about five hundred yards and dismounted to fight again. We nearly reached the enemy's old position on the bluff when we were ordered back to our horses, the firing had ceased and we moved on the road still following the course of the branch with high hills and ridges on either side. The road was of gravel and a very good one. The rumor was that we were going some distance up the river to cross into Virginia. I began to wish that Gen. Morgan would take us to the river so high up that the gunboats could not get at us. We were bothered a great deal by the bushwhackers firing on us from the hills. In several places I saw them walking leisurely along firing and loading. I heard of several persons being wounded by them. We came to a place where the bridge was destroyed. The planks were taken off and hid and the balance burnt. The branch on both sides of the bridge was filled with fallen trees. The water was two or three feet deep and not running. Our only chance was to fill the branch up and make a solid bridge. Our regiment was dismounted to help the sappers and miners. We carried logs, rails, rocks, and dirt, throwing them in the branch till the pile was well out of the water then took the planks of the old bridge and made a good floor on ours. We cut the bank a little and the bridge was completed to the satisfaction of Gen. Morgan who was present. We had worked like Turks making some citizens living near work also. We mounted and moved on. Every mile or so we would come to places where trees were cut across the road. The advance guard would sing out "Sappers and miners to the front! Pass it back!" The sappers and miners would pass us in a jump and go clearing the road. We would hardly stop but pick our way around the obstacle and dash ahead to the next blockade. Sometimes the sappers and miners would be called in front before finishing their last job. We made all the citizens we could catch help clear the road. In this way the command did not have to wait. At last we got ahead of the blockades and double quicked five miles to the town of Chester, Ohio. We halted in the street and dismounted to rest. We opened a store and found a lot of provisions cooked in boxes and baskets that had been cooked for home guards who were to collect to blockade the roads, but we made good use of all the good things. I got two hats, a few yards of cotton and calico, a new curry comb and brush, a hand full of nutmegs, and a few other little tricks. The command coming up, we mounted our horses and moved a square down the street and halted a few minutes. One of the boys went into a grocery and brought us out some hard cider. Then we rode hard till dusk when we halted and dismounted to fight. We were told we were within a half mile of the Ohio River. The advance guard went ahead. We received no orders to move forward so we laid around by our horses and all came near going to sleep.

The General and staff passed us. We mounted our horses and rode quietly down a lane and halted within a hundred yards of the river. We were ordered not to unsaddle or make any noise. We dismounted and sat or lay in the fence corners holding our horses. Everything was quiet except a shot now and then from the advance guard and a scout from the regiment who were after home guards. Three or four squads of prisoners passed us to the rear. A thick fog arose and the night grew very chilly.

I was detailed about midnight with nine others under Lieut. Peddicord to cross the river in a couple of skiffs, and hunt for boats to cross the command in. We went to the river and the fog was so thick that we could not see ten feet in front of us. We could not see how wide the river was or anything about it. We had a citizen with us but he did not give us any information that was satisfactory. We stumbled around there for awhile and the Lieut. Postponed the project till day light. We were chilled through. I could hardly have put a cap on my gun, and we were glad to return to our horses. The boys made a few small rail fires, but were soon ordered to put them out for fear that the Yanks would see them and send a gun boat up and shell us. We could hear the boats puffing away on the river below us. I laid three rails near a deadened fire and slept about ten minutes."

"Sunday, July 19th, 1863. Weather clear. Day light came slow. We went to a stable and got corn for our horses before the fog cleared off. After feeding we rode down the river bank four or five hundred yards to a little village called Portland, Ohio where we dismounted to rest. I went to a house and got some bread and meat. About half of the people had left their houses. I had not been in town more than an hour when a detail of thirty men was called for to strengthen the pickets a few hundred yards below town. Sergeant Miller detailed me for one. We all went to the picket base and halted. We learned that one of our Brigades had taken some earthworks and a piece of artillery a short distance below us. About fifteen prisoners passed to the rear. We were on the river bank. Three of four of us gave our horses in charge of others and went down to the river and took a wash. We heard the boats puffing very plain and hurried to our horses. Buffington Island lay just below us. In five minutes more a shell burst some distance below us. The next one burst nearer on a bee line with us. We knew at once that the Yanks were shelling us. I dismounted and held my horse. The next shell burst right over us about fifty feet high. The boys commenced moving back slow, and I led my horse thinking it safer from the shells. Then two or three of the boats followed us up the river shelling us every few minutes. I saw a shell or solid shot strike the ground within two feet of the heels of a horse in the rear of one of the regiments, giving both horse and rider a shower of dirt. On reaching the hills our regiment bore a little too far to the left and got separated from the rest of the command. Myself, Henry Allen, Sergeant Brown and several others in going through the thick woods and bushes got separated from the regiment. We could hear them ahead of us. Sergeant Brown dropped a bundle and as he was leading an extra horse I dismounted and got it for him. The Yanks getting pretty close in our rear, we moved on. I took the lead. We crossed gullies, climbed steep banks, through thick matted undergrowth that I would have thought impossible to do. I felt proud of my horse for the manner in which he carried me through. In climbing a steep bank a grape vine took off my hat and nearly pulled me off my horse. I had to choose between my hat and my gun which I would loose. I concluded to let the hat go and save my gun and went on without going back for it. I reached an open road and found myself alone. I passed several pieces of our artillery upside down in a ditch with the horses cut loose. I soon found the regiment. A shell or two passed over us about tree top high showing that the Yanks were determined to shell us as long as we were within range. We still had hopes of getting with the balance of the command. The Yanks came up and fired into our rear. Co. A dismounted and fought them till the balance of the regiment reached a rise in the woods, and formed a line. We dismounted to fight and advanced about twenty-five yards. We stood behind trees waiting for the enemy to come up again. There was about two hundred stragglers from other regiments with us. They attempted to get away while we were in line, but they did not go more than a few hundred yards when a sharp fire was opened on them from the front and they came back in a hurry. Nothing coming up in the rear we mounted our horses, but had hardly done so when the Yanks came up and fired into us. We moved back slowly firing a few shots. I saw one Yankee horse loose in the front without a rider. No one hurt on our side. We soon found out that we were surrounded and cut of from the command entirely. Some of the officers by order of Col. Dick Morgan, who had been lost and just got with us, raised a white flag in the shape of a handkerchief on a ram rod. I left the regiment and took a road to the left in hopes of getting away. I did not go far till I met three or four of our boys coming back. They said they had tried to get out on several roads but the Yanks were all around us. I picked up a new hat that was too large for me and went back with them to the regiment. While Col. Dick Morgan was making the conditions of our surrender, we threw away nearly everything we had got on the raid. All of the pistols were thrown as far into the bushes as we could throw them. Some were thrown away in pieces. I met Pa [Burke's father was a member of the same Company] looking as if he had lost something. I laughed and told him that we were trapped and had better make the best of it. Some of the boys even threw away greenbacks and watches for fear that the Yanks would treat them rough if they found such things about them. We cleared our saddles of everything new. There was enough things scatted through the woods to set up quite a respectable variety store. I got a hat to fit me. Most of us put on what ready-made clothing we had on hand. There was some eight or ten left us with the bold intention of cutting their way out. We mounted, took our places, and rode four or five hundred yards down the road handing a Yank our guns as we passed. This made the second gun the Yanks had gotten from me. We came to where two or three regiments of Yankee cavalry and some artillery were in line. We formed two lines in front of them and were counted. The boys gave their spurs to the Yanks standing around. I called a young Yank and told him to take mine off and he did so thanking me for them. We then dismounted and stood in front of our horses. I loosened my saddle girt and slipped my bed comfort out knowing that I would need it to sleep on. I also took my journal from my saddle pockets and wrapped it up in the comfort, feeling very uneasy for its safety. We went through a light examination for arms and were marched into a field nearby in the shade. We silently bid our horses good-by as they were led away. It was very warm and we were all very thirsty. Some of the Yankees took our canteens to a spring and filled them for us. We were impressed with the unwelcome fact that we were no longer at liberty to do as we pleased. We were all in hopes that our being captured would give the rest of the command ample opportunity to escape from the large army in pursuit. Pa came across Lt. J. S. Pankey who before the war was one of his best marble agents in business. Lieut. Pankey said he would do anything he could for us. He appeared a little tipsy and gave me a fifty cent green back bill and would not let me give it back. We then marched through the dust back to our old camp near the river, a distance of three miles, where we found Lieut. Peddicord and a lot more of our boys. We halted in the middle of a wheat field with infantry guards around us. I noticed a good many pieces of artillery, also our own pieces that the yanks got before we could get them out of the bottom. I saw but one of our men dead on the field, but I heard that our loss in killed was five. In an hour or two Cols. Basil Duke and D. Howard Smith with about a hundred more of our command was brought in. The boys were all sorry that Duke was captured, but they cheered him when they found he was unharmed. The yanks issued some fat bacon and army crackers to us, and I picked up one of their haversacks with a tin cup and a spoon in it. I soon silenced all honest scruples and kept them. They were just the things that I needed. The guards and by standers handed us the nearest wheat shocks to sit on and sleep on. I opened three or four bundles of wheat and spread it on the ground myself. Henry White and Leven Young slept on it, and covered with my comfort. It was a warm one and the only thing in the mess in the way of bed clothing. I slept very well.

Statement from Colonel Basil W. Duke, 2nd Kentucky Cavalry, CSA.

"In passing near Pomeroy, there was one continual fight, but, now not with the militia only, for some regular troops made their appearance and took part in the programme. Colonel Grigsby took the lead with the Sixth Kentucky, and dashed through at a gallop, halting when fired on, dismounting his men and dislodging the enemy, and again resuming his rapid march. Major Webber Brought up the rear of the division and held back the enemy, who closed eagerly upon our track."

About 1 o'clock of that day we reached Chester and halted, for an hour and a half, to enable the column to close up, to breathe the horses, and also to obtain a guide, if possible (General Morgan declaring that he would no longer march without one). That halt proved disastrous - it brought us to Buffington ford after night had fallen, and delayed our attempt at crossing until the next morning.

Before quitting Ohio, it is but just to acknowledge the kind hospitality of these last two days. At every house that we approached, the dwellers thereof, themselves absent, perhaps unable to endure a meeting that would have been painful, had left warm pies, freshly baked, upon the tables. This touching attention to our tastes was appreciated. Some individuals were indelicate enough to hint that the pies were intended to propitiate us and prevent the plunder of the houses.

We reached Portland, a little village upon the bank of the river, and a short .distance above Buffington Island, about 8 P. M., and the night was one of solid darkness. General Morgan consulted one or two of his officers upon the propriety of at once attacking an earthwork, thrown up to guard the ford. From all the information he could gather, this work was manned with about three hundred infantry - regular troops - and two heavy guns were mounted in it. Our arrival at this place after dark had involved us in a dilemma. If we did not cross the river that night, there was every chance of our being attacked on the next day by heavy odds. The troops we had seen at Pomeroy were, we at once and correctly conjectured, a portion of the infantry which had been sent after us from Kentucky, and they had been brought by the river, which had risen several feet in the previous week, to intercept us. If transports could pass Pomeroy, the General knew that they could also run up to the bar at Buffington Island. The transports would certainly be accompanied by gun-boats, and our crossing could have been prevented by the latter alone, because our artillery ammunition was nearly exhausted - there was not more than three cartridges to the piece, and we could not have driven off gun-boats with small arms. Moreover, if it was necessary, the troops could march from Pomeroy to Buffington by an excellent road, and reach the latter place in the morning. This they did General Morgan fully appreciated these reasons for getting across the river that night, as did those with whom he advised, but there were, also, very strong reasons against attacking the work at night; and without the capture of the work, which commanded the ford, it would be impossible to cross. The night, as I have stated, was thoroughly dark. Attacks in the dark are always hazardous experiments - in this case it would have been doubly so. We know nothing of the ground, and could not procure guides. Our choice of the direction in which to move to the attack would have been purely guess work. The defenders of the work had only to lie still and fire with artillery and musketry directly to their front, but the assailants would have had a line to preserve, and would have had to exercise great care lest they should fall foul of each other in the obscurity. If this is a difficult business at all times, how much is the danger and trouble increased when it is attempted with broken-down and partially demoralized men?

General Morgan feared, too, that if the attacking party was repulsed, it would come back in such disorder and panic that the whole division would be seriously and injuriously affected. He determined, therefore, to take the work at early dawn and instantly commence the crossing, trusting that it would be effected rapidly and before the enemy arrived. By abandoning the long train of wagons which had been collected, the wounded men, and the artillery, a crossing might have been made, with little difficulty, higher up the river at deeper fords, which we could have readied by a rapid march before the enemy came near them. But General Morgan was determined (after having already hazarded so much) to save all if possible, at the risk of losing all. He ordered me to place two regiments of my brigade in position, as near the earthwork as I thought proper, and attack it at daybreak. I accordingly selected the Fifth and Sixth Kentucky, and formed them about four hundred yards from the work, or from the point where I judged it to be located. Lieutenant Lawrence was also directed to place his Parrots upon a tongue of land projecting northward from a range of hills running parallel with the river. It was intended that he should assist the attacking party, if, for any reason, artillery should be needed. Many efforts were made, during the night, to find other fords, but unsuccessfully.

As soon as the day dawned, the Fifth and Sixth Kentucky were moved against the work, but found it unoccupied. It had been evacuated during the night. Had our scouts, posted to observe it, been vigilant, and had this evacuation, which occurred about two P. M., been discovered and reported, we could have gotten almost the entire division across before the troops coming from Pomeroy arrived. The guns in the work had been dismounted and rolled over the bluff. I immediately sent Gen. Morgan information of the evacuation of the work, and instructed Colonel Smith to take command of the two regiments and move some four or five hundred yards further on the Pomeroy road, by which I supposed that the garrison had retreated. In a few minutes I heard the rattle of musketry in the direction that the regiments had moved, and riding forward to ascertain what occasioned it, found that Colonel Smith had unexpectedly come upon a Federal force advancing upon this road. He attacked and dispersed it, taking forty or fifty prisoners and a piece of artillery, and killing and wounding several. This force turned out to be General Judah's advance guard, and his command was reported to be eight or ten thousand strong, and not far off. Among the wounded was one of his staff, and his Adjutant-General was captured. I instructed Colonel Smith to bring the men back to the ground where they had been formed to attack the work, and rode myself to consult General Morgan and receive his orders. He instructed me to hold the enemy in check, and call for such troops as I might need for that purpose. This valley which we had entered the night before, and had bivouacked in, was about a mile long, and perhaps eight hundred yards wide at the southern extremity (the river runs here nearly due north and south), and gradually narrows toward the other end, until the ridge, which is its western boundary, runs to the water's edge. This ridge is parallel with the river at the southern end of the valley, but a few hundred yards further to the northward both river and ridge incline toward each other. About half way of the valley (equal-distant from either end) the road, by which we had marched from Chester, comes in.

Colonel Smith had posted his men, in accordance with directions given him, at the southern extremity of the valley, with the ridge upon his right flank. At this point the ridge, I should also state, bends almost at right angles to the westward. As I returned from consultation with General Morgan, I found both of the regiments under Colonel Smith in full retreat. When the main body of the enemy (which was now close upon us) appeared, an order had been issued by someone to "rally to horses." While doing this, the line was charged by the enemy's cavalry, of which they had three regiments, two of them, the Seventh and Eighth Michigan, were very fine ones. A detachment of the Fifth Indiana (led by a very gallant officer, Lieutenant O'Neil) headed this charge. The men rallied and turned, as soon as called on to do so, and had no difficulty in driving back the cavalry, but a portion of the Fifth Kentucky was cut off by this charge, and did not take part in the fight which succeeded. These two regiments were not more than two hundred and fifty strong each, and they were dismounted again, and formed across the valley. The Parrot guns had been captured, and, although our line was formed close to them, they were not again in our possession. I sent several couriers to General Morgan, asking for the Second Kentucky, a portion of which I wished to post upon the ridge, and I desired to strengthen the thin, weak line with the remainder. Colonel's Johnson's rear videttes (still kept during the night upon the Chester road) had a short time previously been driven in, and he had formed his brigade to receive the enemy coming from that direction. Colonel Johnson offered me a detachment of his own brigade with which to occupy the part of the ridge immediately upon my right - the necessity of holding it was immediately apparent to him. Believing that the Second Kentucky would soon arrive, I declined his offer.

The force advancing upon the Chester road was General Hobson's, which our late delays had permitted to overtake us. Neither Judah nor Hobson was aware of the other's vicinity, until appraised of it by the sound of their respective guns. We could not have defeated either alone, for Judah was several thousand strong, and Hobson three thousand. We were scarcely nineteen hundred strong, and our ammunition was nearly exhausted - either shot away or worn out in the pouches or cartridge-boxes. The men had on an average, not more than five rounds in their boxes. If, however, either Judah or Hobson had attacked us singly, we could have made good our retreat, in order, and with little loss, [sic]

The attack commenced from both directions, almost simultaneously, and at the same time the gun-boats steamed up and commenced shelling us without fear or favor. I heartily wished that *their* fierce ardor, the result of a feeling of perfect security, could have been subjected to the test of two or three shots through their hulls. They were working, as well as I could judge, five or six guns, Hobson two, and Judah five or six. The shells coming thus from three different directions, seemed to fill the air with their fragments. Colonel Johnson's line, confronting Hobson, was formed at right angles to mine, and upon the level and unsheltered surface of the valley, each was equally exposed to shots aimed at the other. In addition to the infantry deployed in front of my line, the ridge upon the right of it was soon occupied by one of the Michigan regiments, dismounted and deployed as skirmishers. The peculiar formation we were forced to adopt, exposed our entire force engaged to a severe cross fire of musketry. The Second Kentucky and Ninth Tennessee, of the first brigade, were not engaged at all...nor the Eight and Eleventh Kentucky, of the second brigade. These regiments, however, were as completely under fire, in the commencement of the action, as were the others which were protecting the retreat.

The scene in the rear of the lines engaged was one of indescribable confusion. While the bulk of the regiments, which General Morgan was drawing off, were moving from the field in perfect order, there were many stragglers from each, who were circling about the valley in a delirium of fright, clinging instinctively, in all their terror, to bolts of calico and holding on to led horses, but changing the direction in which they galloped, with every shell which

61

whizzed or burst near them. The long train of wagons and ambulances dashed wildly in the only direction which promised escape, and becoming locked and entangled with each other in their flight, many were upset, and terrified horses broke loose from them and plunged wildly through the mass. Some of them in striving to make their way out of the valley, at the northern end, ran afoul of the section of howitzers attached to the second brigade, and guns and wagons were rolled headlong into the steep ravine. Occasionally a solid shot or shell would strike one and bowl it over like a tumbled ten-pin. All this shelling did little damage, and only some twenty-odd men were killed by the musketry - the enemy lost quite as many - but the display of force against us, the cross fire, and our lack of ammunition, seriously disheartened the men, already partially demoralized by the great and unremitted fatigue.

The left flank of my line, between which and the river there was an interval of at least three hundred yards, was completely turned, and the Sixth Kentucky was almost surrounded. This regiment (under the command of Major William Bullitt, an officer of the calmest and most perfect bravery), behaved nobly. It stood the heavy attack of the enemy like a bastion. At length seeing that General Morgan had gotten out of the valley with the rest of the division, Colonel Johnson and myself, upon consultation, determined to withdraw simultaneously. We had checked this superior force for more than half an hour - which, as much as our assailants boasted of their victory, was quite as good as an equal number of the best of them could have done against such odds.

The men were remounted without confusion, and retreated in column of fours from right of companies, and for quite a mile in perfect order. The Sixth Kentucky formed to the "rear into line" three times, and with empty guns, kept the pursuing cavalry at bay. But when we neared the other end of the valley and saw that there were but two avenues of escape from it - the men broke ranks and rushed for them. In a moment, each was blocked. The gunboats sought to rake these roads with grape - and although they aimed too high to inflict much injury, the hiss of the dreaded missiles increased the panic. The Seventh Michigan soon came up and dashed pell-mell into the crowd of fugitives. Colonel Smith, Captain Campbell, Captain Thorpe, and myself, and some fifty other officers and men, were forced by the charge of this regiment into a ravine on the left of the road and soon afterward captured. Captain Thorpe saved me from capture at an earlier date, only to ultimately share my fate. He had acted as Adjutant General of the First Brigade, since the detachment of Captain Davis, and had performed all of his duties with untiring assiduity and perfect efficiency. On this day, there was allowed opportunity for the display of courage only, and for that he was ever distinguished.

About seven hundred prisoners were taken from us in this fight. Among the officers captured were Colonels Ward and Morgan, Lieutenant Colonel Huffman, who was also severely wounded, and Majors Bullock and Bullitt.

Notes, Telegrams, Statements and Facts

Telegraph from Athens, Ohio to General Burnside:

July 18, 1863
General Burnside:

I have obtained the following from the military committee:

We sent out yesterday at 4 p.m. 100 men with axes, under Lieutenant Long, Seventh Ohio Cavalry, with 50 scouts, to impede Morgan's progress; also 250 armed men from our county to their support. We have had dispatches from our front this fore-noon, saying that Morgan was moving on line of road through Rutland to Pomeroy. Our forces expected that they would move to get on his front in case he moved to go up river. Colonel Gilmore's forces moved from here this morning at 3 a. m. on the line of our force. Will have 50 mounted men here waiting our orders, and we are all the time at our headquarters, and will forward any dispatches you may wish to any point desired.

M. M. Greene
Chairman, Athens County Military Committee

Telegraph from General Burnside in Cincinnati to Captain Barringer in Parkersburg:

July 18, 1863, Cincinnati, Ohio

Capt. Barringer:

Keep the boats on your side of the river, and let nothing pass below for the present. Send messenger to Conine, asking him to scour the country well, and urge the blockading of the roads from Big Hocking to Athens. Will telegraph Colonel Wallace.

A. E. Burnside,
Major-General

Telegraph from General Burnside to General Hobson:

July 18, 1863, Cincinnati, Ohio

General Hobson:

Push your command to the utmost of its capacity. If you can overtake Morgan with half your force, I am satisfied you can whip him. Judah ought to have been in front of Morgan, but stopped at Centreville last night. Left there this morning at 5 in pursuit. Send message by this courier.

A. E. Burnside,
Major-General

Telegraph from General Burnside to General Manson in Portsmouth:

July 18, 1863, Cincinnati, Ohio

General Manson:

Have any of your command gone up the river? Am I to understand that Judah was at Centreville last night with his whole force, and was to leave there this morning at 5? Did you leave any of your command with him? Telegraph all you know of the position of the enemy. It was reported at Pomeroy that he was at Rutland at 2 this morning.

A. E. Burnside,
Major-General

Telegraph from Captain A. A. Hunter at Gallipolis to General Burnside:

July 18, 1863, Gallipolis, Ohio

General Burnside:

A part of Morgan's forces camped 15 miles from here last night. He is supposed to be in neighborhood of Pomeroy. General Scammon, with a portion of his command, left here early this morning. Three gunboats above. Re-enforcements, infantry and artillery, en route from the Kanawha. I can hold this place. Hobson and Judah about 10 miles behind Morgan. He will likely be surrounded tomorrow, if line is closed between Hamden and Athens.

A. A. Hunter,
Captain, Commanding Post

Telegraph from General Judah at Pomeroy to General Burnside:

July 18, 1863, Pomeroy, Ohio

Major General Burnside:

I marched all night from Portsmouth, and continued to Centreville yesterday. Morgan's Advance got to within 4 miles of me ignorantly, then fell back, and made for Keystone Furnace, Rutland, and Chester. I pushed on to this place, 30 miles, where I arrived two hours since. Hobson is on this side of Rutland. All information assures me that Morgan passed Chester some three hours since, for Buffington Island. So certain that I sent word to Hobson to push on all that can keep up in track of enemy, via Chester. I move in less than one hour to Buffington, via Racine, my best road. Moving thus, Morgan is in a trap, from which he can't escape. I think I will be able to telegraph you his defeat tomorrow morning, should he have taken the route I am almost certain he has. A prisoner, who has been with Morgan all day, and released and came on foot from Chester, tells me that Morgan thinks Hobson has given out and given up pursuit. He does not know my position. He thinks he can manage the gunboats with his 10-pounder pieces. Scammon has gone from here to Buffington. I have sent boat to Gallipolis for rations for Hobson and myself.

Telegram from Captain A.V. Barringer to General Burnside:

July 18, 1863, Parkersburg, West Virginia

One of my messengers just in, and reports Morgan at Chester, 26 miles from here, and 5 miles from Pomeroy, at 4 p.m. Four hundred militia went down to Buffington, with artillery, yesterday. Lieutenant Conine is at Little Hocking Bridge, with 1,200 men. I have no steamboat; expecting one down hourly, from Pittsburg, drawing 30 inches, the ferry-boat, drawing 26 inches, is at Blennerhassett's Island, helping off steamer Eagle, which draws 36 inches. Stores all in Parkersburg, on Virginia side. Can use floats, if necessary, to help artillery or men.

A. V. Barringer,
Captain, and Commissary of Subsistence

A typical U.S. River Gunboat similar to the USS Moose

Fitch's Battle Report

U.S.S. Moose,
Buffington Island, July 19, 1863.

SIR: I have the honor to state that since my last reports regarding Morgan, I have followed on up the river, keeping on his right. In some instances I was compelled to get out warps to get over falls, shoals, and swift water, but I had determined to cut him off at all hazards. This morning I had the good fortune to intercept him just above this island, making for the river and attempting to ford. I at once engaged him, drove him from the banks, and captured two pieces of his artillery, a portion of his baggage train, horses, small arms, etc. During this time General Judah was pressing on his rear.

He did not engage us over an hour, when his forces broke in the utmost confusion, throwing away their arms and clothing and taking to the hills. A portion, however, moved up along the bank in hasty retreat, but I followed them so closely that they soon broke and disappeared up the ravines and over the hills. In this column moving up along the bank were several buggies and carriages, which were abandoned to us. One of the carriages, in which Morgan was said to be riding, was upset by one of our shell, and both horses disabled. The road along the bank was literally strewn with his plunder, such as cloth, boots, shoes, small arms, and the like, but I had not time to land and take possession of these things, as I wished to keep on up the river with the remnant of his scattered band, knowing that General Judah would look out for those left in the rear. About 15 miles above this point, I again fell in with another portion of his forces fording; the current was so very swift and the channel so narrow, that it was some time before I could get within range of them. As soon as possible I opened fire on them, killing 2 and causing many of the horses to leave their riders in the water. Some had already got across, but many put back and again took up the river. It was reported afterwards that some 25 or 30 were drowned. I left standing on both banks some 15 or 20 horses without riders, but had not time to stop for them. Pushing on up the river, I again saw another squad of some 25 or 30 crossing, but could not, in consequence of very shoal and swift water, get within range of them till they had crossed.

Having reached as high as it was safe for me to venture at this stage of water, and the river still falling, I dropped down below Burlington Island, where I will remain till morning, and then proceed below Letart Falls.

Although I could get but two vessels the Moose and Alleghany Belle) in the engagement today, owing to the numerous shoals and shape of the river, yet I can testify to the energetic, prompt, and efficient part the officers and crews of the steamers Reindeer, Naumkeag, Victory, and Springfield took in the chase. The officers and crew of this vessel and the Alleghany Belle acted in the most commendable manner, and although many of them had never before been under fire, they did their duty well.

I know not the number of killed, wounded, and prisoners, but am told the enemy suffered severely, and that nearly the entire force was captured.

Very respectfully, your obedient servant,
LEROY FITCH,
Lieutenant-Commander.

Diary Entry of Captain Thomas Coombs, 5th Kentucky Cavalry, CSA:

"From the 9th until the 19th through Indiana and Ohio was almost a continual skirmish day & night with Soldiers, Home Guards, & Citizens. We marched very hard and fast, breaking down our horses and procuring fresh ones. On the night of the 18th of July we reached the Ohio River at Buffington Bar and found a wide, deep and unfordable river, rapidly rising. We could not cross in the Stygian Darkness by which we were surrounded, and sinking down upon its shores, exhausted nature found repose in sleep."

Diary Entry of Private John Weatherred, 9th Tennessee Cavalry, CSA:

"In passing near Pomeroy, Ohio on the 18th of July, we had to fight at every cross road and every joint where the Blue Boys could find a good position to fight us and they were regular, who had come up by boats to Pomeroy from Cincinnati and had come out on every road from Pomeroy to fight us. After passing this the road ran through a deep ravine for 4 or 5 miles. We were fired on from the hills about all the way through. About 1 p. m. we reached Chester where we stopped for about two hours. This stop brought us to the Village of Portland on the Banks of the Ohio; a short distant above Buffington Island about 8 p. m. and the night was very dark and we remained all night holding our horses by the bridle reigns. Sleeping and talking and saying to one another often we would wake up at intervals through the night. That if we stay here until morning we will be surrounded and many of us will be captured."

Diary Entry of Captain Theodore F. Allen, 7th Ohio Cavalry, USA.

"Just as the sky was growing gray with coming dawn on July 19th the welcome sound of half a dozen shots by our advanced guard told us we had struck Morgan's outpost. Colonel Kautz immediately pushed his command forward at a brisk gait. Debouching from the river hills into the valley of the Ohio, near Buffington Island, we developed Morgan's force where it had been delayed by fog, waiting for daylight to ford the river into West Virginia. Morgan's two thousand horsemen were waiting on the lower end of a valley that lay between the hills and the river. The Union troops under General Judah, coming up the river from Pomeroy, where the steamboats had landed them, approached the enemy about the same time our vanguard of General Hobson's force, led by Colonel Kautz, began the decent into the middle of the valley occupied by Morgan. Colonel Kautz attacked immediately upon arrival; our two pieces of artillery, answering Judah's guns, informed Morgan that those who had followed him from the Cumberland River had closed in on him."

Telegram from General Judah at Buffington Island to General Burnside July 19, 1863:

Major General Burnside:

Agreeably with my promise by telegraph last night, I announce the defeat of Morgan's force. I traveled all night from Pomeroy; reached Buffington Flats at 5:30 this morning. A dense fog pervades everything. I took a small advance guard, and, with my escort, advanced with my staff, to reconnoiter down a road surrounded by enclosed fields. I had proceeded cautiously but one-fourth of a mile, when I found myself surrounded by the enemy, in front and on my flanks, dismounted, who poured in a heavy fire. Before I could get a piece of artillery in position it was captured. Two men were killed–Major McCook and Lieutenant Price–and some enlisted men wounded; Captain Kise, assistant adjutant-general, and Captain Grafton, volunteer aide-de-camp, with about 30 men, were captured. Finding it impossible to resist the heavy force of three regiments brought up against me, led by Basil Duke, I retreated upon the main body, brought it into action, and, in less than half an hour, completely routed the enemy. I recaptured the piece I lost; captured large quantities of camp equipage, two pieces of the enemy's artillery, and forced him to abandon the only three he had left, driving him upon General Hobson. Particulars given more fully in report. Large number of prisoners taken. Enemy's loss not yet ascertained; it cannot fall short of 100 killed and wounded.

H. M. Judah,
Brigadier-General

Statement from Private George Dallas Mosgrove, 4th Kentucky Cavalry, CSA:

"In the early morning General Morgan rode into the river, but when about half way across, seeing that the greater number of his men would be forced to remain on the Ohio shore, he turned and rode back to that side of the stream, resolved to share the fate of his men.

Accompanying the raiders were a number of active and intelligent colored boys serving their young masters, to whom they were singularly devoted. Among them was a little fellow named "Box," a privileged character, whose impudent airs were condoned by the cavaliers in consideration of his uniform cheerfulness and enlivening plantation melodies. When General Morgan had returned to the Ohio shore he saw Box plunge into the river and boldly swim toward the other side. Fearing the little fellow would be drowned, The General called him to return. "No, Marse John," cried Box, "if dey ketch you dey may parole you, but if dey ketch dis nigger in a free State he ain't a-gwine ter git away while de wah lasts." Narrowly missing collision with a gunboat, Box crossed the river all right and escaped southward to the old plantation."

Diary Entry of Private Charles W. Durling, 45th Ohio Infantry, USA.

"Sunday, July 19

Still pressing hard on Johnny. Came up with him about noon. Capture over 1000 prisoners at eight mile island."

Diary Entry of Captain Theodore F. Allen, 7th Ohio Cavalry, USA:

"The one desperate chance of escape was by the road leading out of the upper end of the valley, and towards this Morgan's confused troopers swept through the standing grain fields of the fertile farm lands, with Colonel Kautz's command in hot pursuit."

Diary Entry of Lt. Colonel James B. McCrary, 11th Kentucky Cavalry, CSA:

"July 18 – 19. All are on the 'qui vive,' for the Ohio River is full of gunboats and transports, and an immense force of cavalry is hovering in our rear. We reached Buffington tonight. All was quiet. A dense fog wrapped this woodland scene. Early in the morning of the 19th the Yankees guarding the ford were attacked by our force, and driven away and their artillery captured. Immediately after this, and whilst we were trying the river to ascertain if it was fordable, the gunboats steamed up the river. The transports landed their infantry, thousands of cavalry moved down upon us, and the artillery commenced its deadly work. We formed and fought here to no purpose. The river was very full inconsequence of a heavy rain away up the river. Shells and Minnie balls were ricocheting and exploding in every direction, cavalry were charging and the infantry with its slow, measured tread moved upon us, while broadside after broadside was poured upon our doomed command from the gunboats. It seemed as if our comparatively small command would be swallowed up by the innumerable hordes. About half of it was captured or killed. I made my way out by charging through the enemy's lines with about one-half the Regiment, and finally formed a juncture with the remnant of our command under Gen Morgan, now numbering 1,200. With these we moved toward Cheshire, traveling rapidly all night, passing around the enemy's pickets, over cliffs and ravines, which, under ordinary circumstances, would have been considered insurmountable."

Diary Entry of Captain Thomas Coombs, 5th Kentucky Cavalry, CSA:

"The first streak of morning light aroused us from our weary slumbers and mounting our tired and starving horses we prepared to meet the enemy, who in overwhelming numbers were rapidly closing around us, and several Gun Boats Gun Boats had ascended the river immediately in our front. We fought until our ammunition was expended and then retreated up the river, losing three or four hundred men; among them Cols. Duke, Smith & Morgan. I now had the command of our right & moving 9 m. up the river we again attempted to cross. Col. Johnson with about 300 men succeeded, but Gen. Morgan with the main body of the Comd. was nearly all night and making a wide detour on the 20th of July at 4 P.M. we arrived at Cheshire, O., on the river some 50 or 60 miles below Buffington. For several hours previous to arriving at Cheshire the 5th Ky. under my Comd. & the 6th Comd. by R. D. Logan were actively engaged with Woolford's and Judah's Cavalry that hotly pressed our rear. Ammunition being entirely exhausted, and one-half the command having lost their guns during the rapid retreat of the preceding day and night, and the river being impassable, we were forced to surrender. We held a Council of War on a high hill about 4 mi. below Cheshire and sent a flag of truce to Col. Coleman, of Cluke's Regt. Was our senior officer left, & the terms of surrender was agreed about sunset."

Statement from Private George Dallas Mosgrove, 4th Kentucky Cavalry, CSA:

"With about one thousand gallant but hopeless men, General Morgan withdrew from the Melee at Buffington Island and rode eastward, closely pursued by Hobson's indefatigable cavalry. Weary and harassed, the Confederate chieftain continued to elude his relentless pursuers for six days, when, his followers reduced to two hundred men, he surrendered, July 26th, to a detachment of Hobson's Kentucky Cavalrymen – Greek against Greek."

Statement from General Basil W. Duke, 2nd Kentucky Cavalry, CSA:

"The dreaded missiles passed overhead and their hiss increased the panic. A shell struck the road throwing up a cloud of dust. Troopers began unloading their booty of the raid. Shoes, parasols, skates, birdcages were scatted to the wind. Long bolts of muslin and calico spun out in banners of brilliant colors, streaming in the morning sunlight. The wounded and terror-stricken occupants of the ambulance wagons urged the scared horses into headlong flight. Often they became locked together and were hurdled over as if by an earthquake. Occasionally a solid shot or unexploded shell would strike one, and dash it into splinters. The remaining section of Confederate artillery tumbled into a ravine as if the guns had been as light as feathers. The gunboats raked the road with grapeshot. In a moment the panic was complete and the disaster irretrievable."

Diary Entry of Captain Theodore F. Allen, 7th Ohio Cavalry, USA:

"Immediately after the stampede began each one of Morgan's troopers began to unload the plunder carried on his horse – boots, shoes, stockings, gloves, skates, sleigh bells, and bird cages scattered to the winds. Then the flying horsemen let loose their bolts of muslin and calico; holding one end, each cavalryman let the whole hundred yards stream out behind him. The most gorgeous kaleidoscopic view imaginable would not serve to describe the retreat of this 'army with banners,' and instantly, though greatly to our surprise, we found ourselves to be rainbow chasers in almost the literal sense of the word. No road could accommodate such a confused mass of two thousand flying horsemen, and they spread across the narrowing valley. Across the upper end of the valley a stream came down out of the hills to the river, cutting its way through the plain in a deep gorge. Into this gorge plunged and piled the flying cavalry, with their wagons of plunder, and our force close behind them. Some succeeded in getting beyond this sunken gorge to continue their flight, though many, dismounted and disabled, were captured here, while some halted a short distance beyond in the forest-clad hills to surrender, rather than continue a hopeless flight."

Diary Entry of Private John Weatherred, 9th Tennessee Cavalry, CSA:

"About 350 of the boys crossed the river some distance above Buffington Island in the afternoon of July 19th under the command of Col. Adam R. Jackson (Johnson)."

Statement from Colonel Adam. R. Johnson, 10th Kentucky Cavalry, CSA:

"Looking back across the river I saw a number of hats floating on the surface, and knew that each represented a brave and gallant Confederate who had found a watery grave..."

Fact: The Battle of Buffington Island was the only significant Civil War battle fought in the State of Ohio.

Fact: Three future Presidents took part in the Battle of Buffington Island. James Garfield, Rutherford B. Hayes, and William McKinley.

Fact: From the Official Records of the War Department military casualties due to Morgans' Raid are:
USA.-22 Killed, 80 wounded, 26 Missing, 790 captured.
CSA.-86 Killed, 385 wounded, 3000 missing or captured.

Fact: Almost 4,400 Ohioans filed claims for compensation with the federal government for items that they lost to the Confederates during the raid. The claims amounted to $678,915, with the government authorizing compensation in the amount of $576,225.

Fact: USS Moose description:

Displacement: 189 tons

Length: 154 ft 8 in (47.14 m)

Beam: 32 ft 2 in (9.80 m)

Draft: 5 ft (1.5 m)

Propulsion: steam engine stern wheel-propelled

Speed: 6 knots

Armament: six 24-pounder guns

The Fighting McCooks

Daniel McCook and eight of his nine sons took up arms for the North, as did his brother, John McCook, and his five sons. Individually, the two families were known as the Tribe of Dan and the Tribe of John. Together, they came to be referred to as the "Fighting McCooks".

Daniel McCook, the patriarch of the Tribe of Dan, lived in Carrolton, Ohio, before the Civil War. He received a commission as major and lost his life in the Battle of Buffington Island in 1863. George McCook, Dan's son, was a brigadier-general and served as an Ohio attorney general before the Civil War. Other members of the Tribe of Dan included Latimer, Robert, Alexander, Daniel, Jr., Edwin Stanton, Charles Morris, and John James. Latimer attained the rank of major. Confederate guerrillas murdered him while he lay wounded in the back of an ambulance in Tennessee during 1862. Robert rose to the rank of brigadier-general and also died in Tennessee. Alexander became a major general and survived the war. Edwin also was a major general. Although wounded severely three times in the conflict, Edwin survived the war. He eventually became the governor of the North Dakota Territory and was assassinated. Daniel McCook became a brigadier-general and was killed in 1864 at the Battle of Kennesaw Mountain. Charles Morris was the first McCook killed in the war, dying from wounds he received at the First Battle of Bull Run. John James survived the war with the rank of colonel.

The Tribe of John included the family patriarch, John McCook. A doctor in Steubenville before the war, he served as a volunteer surgeon during the Civil War. Other members of the Tribe of John included Edward, Anson, Henry, John James, and Roderick. All members of the Tribe of John survived the Civil War. Edward and Anson were major generals. Henry and John James were lieutenants and served as chaplains in the Union Army. Roderick became a commander in the United States Navy.

Fourteen of the McCooks became officers. Four of them died in service to their country. The Fighting McCooks' dedication to the Union war effort made them well known in the North.

Major Daniel McCook Sr.
Killed at the Battle of Buffington Island

The Deaths of Pulliam Halliday Hysell and Dr. William Hudson.

On Saturday, July 18, 1863, General John Hunt Morgan and his band of Confederate Raiders had just left the town of Rutland in Meigs County. They were enroute to Buffington Island near the Meigs County town of Portland to cross the Ohio River and make their escape into West Virginia. The river was shallow there and had been previously checked out by Morgan's advance scouts weeks earlier. The Union forces were rapidly gaining on Morgan and he was desperately seeking alternate places to cross the river. In Rutland they found the town blacksmith, Joseph Giles, hiding in a cellar and took him prisoner. They asked him where they could cross the river and he said Middleport had a ferry service and he could cross there. Morgan's men forced Giles to lead them there. They never made it to Middleport as they ran into heavily fortified positions held by the local militia and militia from Marietta blocking their way. They decided to go back to their original plan of crossing at Buffington Island and this diversion cost the life of one of my ancestors.

Pulliam Halliday Hysell (Hisle) was my second Cousin, 5 times removed. He was born in Culpepper County, Virginia in the year 1798. He immigrated to Ohio along with numerous other family members. In 1817 he married Nancy Woodward. They had ten children. His first son, Pulliam M. Halliday Hysell, was born in 1817. His son enlisted in the Union Army in 1861 and served with the Seventh Independent Battery, Ohio Light Artillery.

On that fateful day in 1863, Pulliam Halliday Senior who had been drinking all day, saw the Raiders coming up the road from Rutland towards Middleport, passing in front of his house. He went out on his front porch and began shouting at the Rebels as they filed by. He was cursing them, calling them names and screaming insults at them. His neighbor, Doctor William Hudson, who lived across the road from him, heard the commotion and was on the way over to the Hysell house to try to quiet the old man down and get him out of harm's way. He didn't make it. A rebel trooper shot and killed Pulliam Halliday Hysell as he stood in defiance on his porch. The doctor, who was 74 years old, took off running and the trooper shot him also. He was mortally wounded and died about a week later.

A Statement of Interest

I grew up in the town of Tuppers Plains, Meigs County, Ohio back in the 1960's. When I was a young boy, I decided to teach myself how to play the guitar I had just received from my brother. I got an old Hank Williams "Teach Yourself to Play" book and started practicing. Two of my best friends were Johnny and Ronny Dodderer who lived just outside of town on route 681 from Tuppers Plains towards Reedsville. They had an older brother named David who was quite an accomplished guitar player and one day I was invited to bring my guitar out to their home and play along with him and maybe learn something.

The house the Dodderer's lived in was very old, I found out many years later from one of their cousins, Bill Dodderer that it had actually started out as a log cabin built by the first Dodderer who settled there back in 1812. (I can't remember his name.) It had been added on to until it was a two story home. The Dodderer's had one of the finest springs I ever heard of. The water from their spring was so sweet and cold. Bill said that is why the first Dodderer chose that spot to settle.

Back to the visit…When I arrived at the Dodderer's we began playing songs and I was picking up a few things from David. We decided to take a break and the father, Mr. Roland Dodderer and I started talking about the Civil War and Morgan's Raiders. He told me that after Morgan and his men failed to cross the river on their second try at Reedsville, they headed back towards Tuppers Plains and that they camped on a hillside, "Just over yonder". The Rebs tried to sleep there but the Union Cavalry was hot on their heels and when daybreak came, the Rebs just jumped on their horses and took off, leaving a lot of stuff behind there on that hillside. Roland told me that his father (or grandfather) went over to that hillside and gathered up all kinds of stuff the Rebs had unloaded. Roland went up stairs and came back down carrying a small saddle with the initials CSA on it, a set of spurs and an old pistol. He gave me an old minie ball that had turned white with age and told me to keep it. I carried that minie ball for years and years as a good luck piece until I lost it somewhere.

The reason I told you this story is to corroborate the next one. Another one of my good friends at Tuppers Plains was Gary Hostetter. Gary lived with his Grandmother, Mabel, in an old house that was located just outside of town on Route 681 towards Reedsville. During my Senior year at Eastern High School, in 1966, my parents moved to Racine. I did not want to change schools so I would either use my Dad's car to commute to Eastern or just stay with friends and their generous parents in the Tuppers Plains area. I spent a lot of time with the Brooks and Landon Families. Gary was the greatest guy. He would chauffer me around, and a lot of times take me back and forth between Racine and Tuppers Plains and wouldn't take a dime for it.

While in High School I enlisted in the U.S. Navy and after I graduated I was to report for boot camp. I was to catch a bus at an un-Godly hour in Parkersburg. Gary volunteered to drive me up there so my Parents wouldn't have to. I spent the night at Gary's house. As usual his Grandmother and I talked about the old days. I would love to hear her stories about the pioneer days. I wish I could remember them, or had written them down. I do remember her telling me about some of her family being captured by Indians (They originally settled around Springfield, Ohio and the Urbana area.) and they were rescued by Simon Kenton.

Gary and I got up very early the next morning and Mabel was already up fixing us a breakfast. She was a super nice lady. She asked me if I slept well. I answered "yes" and she said, "I thought you would like sleeping in the General's room… he slept in that same bed too." I was confused and asked, "What General?" Thinking she may be talking about one of her family members. She then told me that right after the Battle of Buffington Island, Morgan and his men came to Tuppers Plains. At that time, this house was just finished being built by her father (or grandfather). Morgan and some of his staff came to the house and took it over for the night. General Morgan slept in the same small bedroom next to the kitchen area that I did. He didn't stay long. Just a few winks of sleep and he was up and on his way as the Union forces were right behind him.

I have no doubt that what Mabel told me is the truth. Knowing this wonderful lady and her character, I can safely say that she would never have told me this story if it were not true.

Steve Badgley
Canal Winchester, Ohio

(Photo provided by Chester Bruce Hagar, Tuppers Plains, Ohio.)

Postscript:

In the 19th and early 20th centuries, the family spelled their name Hostottle. Some later family members changed it to Hostetter.

The lady holding the horses in this picture is believed to be Joanna (Bibbee) Hostottle, wife of David Hostottle. The man is believed to be one of her brothers and his wife.

The First Raider

The first Raider to carry the Confederate flag onto Ohio soil was not General Morgan. It was actually Brigadier General Albert Jenkins. On September 4, 1862, Jenkins and a little over 500 raiders crossed the river at Buffington Island. From there they travelled west and attacked the town of Racine where they stole 25 horses and re-crossed the river back into West Virginia.

Brigadier General
Albert G. Jenkins
8th Virginia Cavalry CSA
1st Ohio Raider

Pictures of interest

Brigadier General
John Hunt Morgan
CSA

Major-General
Ambrose E. Burnside
Commander of the Army of The Ohio

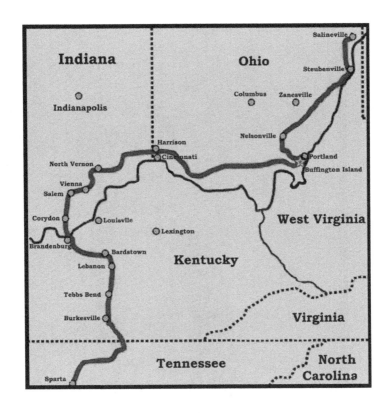

Map of Morgan's Raid

General
Henry M. Judah
Commander 3rd Division of the XXIII Corps

Home of Tunis Middleswart
Near Portland
Morgan commandered this house as his headquarters.

Colonel
James. M. Shackelford
8th Kentucky Volunteer Infantry
USA

Brigadier General
Edward H. Hobson
13th Kentucky Infantry USA

Captain
Ralph Sheldon
2nd Kentucky Cavalry, CSA

Captain
Thomas Henry Hines
9th Kentucky Cavalry

Col. Adam R. Johnson
10th Kentucky Cavalry, CSA

Portland, Ohio
From an old tintype photo taken from across the river in West Virginia

The Williamson House
Used as a field hospital during the Battle of Buffington Island

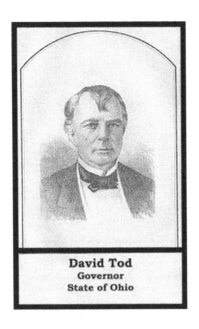

David Tod
Governor
State of Ohio

A typical U.S. River Gunboat similar to the USS Moose

Colonel
Richard C. "Dick" Morgan
14th Kentucky Cavalry CSA
Brother of General Morgan

Lt. Col W. W. Ward

Private
George Ellsworth
"Lightning"

2nd Kentucky Cavalry CSA
Morgan's Telegrapher

Lt. Colonel
James B. McCreary

11th Kentucky Cavalry
Later 37th Governor of Kentucky

Private
G. W. Bowman
2nd Kentucky Cavalry CSA

Some of Morgan's captured officers in prison playing cards.

$1,000!
REWARD.

Head Quarters U. S. Forces,
Columbus, O., Nov. 28, 1863.

GEN. JOHN H. MORGAN
Captains J. C. Bennett, L. B. Taylor, L. D. Hockersmith, Sheldon T. H. Haines, and G. S. Magee,

Escaped from the Ohio Penitentiary on the night of the 27th instant.

A Reward of $1,000!

Will be paid for the apprehension and arrest of John Morgan, and a suitable reward for the apprehension and arrest of the others.

WM. WALLACE,
Colonel 15th O. V. I. Commanding.

For more great stories from our past, please visit our web site.

Badgley Publishing Company

WWW.BadgleyPublishingCompany.com

Made in the USA
Monee, IL
13 August 2020